IMAGES
of America

F.E. WARREN AIR FORCE BASE

ON THE COVER: Troops standing at attention had been a common sight on this military installation for over 100 years. In 1910, unidentified guard mount troops are standing on review in their full dress uniforms with gloves and dress hats on Argonne Parade Field in front of Pershing Boulevard. The guardhouse and barracks are behind them. (WSA.)

IMAGES
of America

F.E. WARREN AIR FORCE BASE

Paula Bauman Taylor

ARCADIA PUBLISHING

ISBN 978-0-7385-9226-8

Published by Arcadia Publishing
Charleston, South Carolina

Library of Congress Control Number: 2011939214

For all general information, please contact Arcadia Publishing:
Telephone 843-853-2070
Fax 843-853-0044
E-mail sales@arcadiapublishing.com
For customer service and orders:
Toll-Free 1-888-313-2665

Visit us on the Internet at www.arcadiapublishing.com

Lovingly dedicated to my husband, Jim Taylor, and my children, Daniek and James Taylor

Contents

Acknowledgments

I would like to thank F.E. Warren Air Force Base for the use of photographs for this book. Many thanks go to Mike Byrd, the 90th Missile Wing historian, for his support, locating and scanning in photographs, information, and friendship; the 90th Missile Wing Civil Engineer Squadron and personnel Natalie Gorecki, Lori Ford, and Travis Beckwith; 90th Security Forces Military Working Dog Section; MSgt. Dan Lyon for the information and research he did and for reviewing the book; the 90th Missile Wing public affairs office and Barry Kistler, the 90th Missile Wing director of staff, for the opportunity to write this book; and to friends who have supported me—Sheila Beavers, Shawn and Jeff Bowell.

I would also like to thank the Wyoming State Archives, Department of State Parks and Cultural Resources, for its archives, photographs used in this book, and the efficient help of its records reference archivist Suzi Taylor.

I wish to thank my family for their hard work on this project: my husband, Jim Taylor; my twins, James Taylor and Daniek Taylor; and my mother, Leola Bauman. I owe a special thanks to my sister, Debra Bauman Brown, who gave her valuable time to help with the complete process in writing this book.

The photographs used from F.E. Warren Air Force Base will be identified as FEW. The photographs used from the Wyoming State Archives, Department of State Parks and Cultural Resources, will be identified as WSA. Several images were used from the J.E. Stimson Collection, Wyoming State Archives, Department of State Parks and Cultural Resources, and will be identified by WSA, Stimson.

Introduction

F.E. Warren is the oldest continuously active base in the Air Force system. It has been open as a military facility since 1867, when the Army established the post to protect the railroad as it was being built through the Dakota Territory. Both the city of Cheyenne, Wyoming, and the fort were platted on July 4, 1867, by Gen. Grenville Dodge and Gen. Christopher Augur. The original name for the post was Fort D.A. Russell, after Gen. David A. Russell, a Civil War hero who had died at the Third Battle of Winchester. The first commander of the new post was Gen. John D. Stevenson, 30th Infantry. This military installation has had three different names over the years: Fort D.A. Russell (1867–1929), Fort F.E. Warren (1930–1949), and F.E. Warren Air Force Base (1949–present). The first unit to arrive at the post was the 30th Infantry, which marched from Omaha, Nebraska. Within two months, the 2nd Cavalry Unit showed up, camping out in military pup tents until the first wooden structures were built. In 1885, the US Department of War designated Fort Russell a permanent post due to its strategic location. The original wooden buildings were replaced with brick structures.

During the Spanish-American War, the post became a major mobilization point. In a reorganization of the military following the war, and thanks to Sen. Francis E. Warren, the post once again was declared a permanent installation and brought to brigade size. It was at this time that Pole Mountain, consisting of approximately 36,800 acres west of the post, was established as a target and maneuvering range. After the turn of the 20th century, there were many noted military men stationed at the post. The Air Force recognizes Gen. William "Billy" Mitchell as the "Father of Air Power." Gen. Mark Clark was the Allied commandeering officer in Italy during World War II. Gen. Benjamin O. Davis was the first African American to become a general in the US Army. Also, Dr. Walter Reed spent time at the post during this period.

During World War I, the fort would again become a mobilization point and a training base for field artillery units. Thus began artillery training on the post. The lone runway found on base was built for airmail. In 1919, it was the only time World War I flying ace Eddie Rickenbacker ever crashed his plane.

Francis E. Warren passed away in November 1929, and the military changed the name from Fort D.A. Russell to Fort Francis E. Warren in his memory. At the onset of American involvement in World War II, a Quartermaster Training Center was established. Within six months, 282 temporary frame buildings were constructed to house a garrison of 20,000 soldiers. Along with this training center, a prisoner-of-war camp was established, which would ultimately house over 3,560 German and Italian prisoners. In 1943, the last military horse left the post when it was mechanized.

In 1947, when the Air Force was created, the fort became an Air Force base. During the first 13 years as an Air Force facility, the mission was training troops in the Air Training Command. The first training unit assigned to the post was the 463rd Air Force Base Unit, the Aviation Engineer School. On May 15, 1948, that school was re-designated as the US Air Force Technical School. Soon, the 463rd was reorganized into the 3450th Technical Training Wing on August 28, 1948.

Automotive training, a research laboratory to study rheumatic fever and respiratory ailments, and Fixed Wire Communication Training were added later that year. For the third time, the post would receive a new name. On July 7, 1949, the name changed from Fort Francis E. Warren to Francis E. Warren Air Force Base. The main mission of the base was to serve as a technical training school. At times, total base personnel would exceed 12,000 troops. Although the base did not have a runway, there were aircraft assigned to the wing. One B-25, several C-47s, and T-6s were housed at the Cheyenne Municipal Airport for the wing's use.

Since the 1950s, the mission of the base has been deterrence by utilizing intercontinental ballistic missiles (ICBMs). F.E. Warren would be the first base to have operational Atlas missiles. The 4320th Strategic Missile Wing was activated on February 1, 1958, but was soon changed to the 706th Strategic Missile Wing. There were three squadrons—549th, 564th, and 565th—assigned to the first Atlas D missiles. The 564th became the first operational ICBM unit in the recently assigned Strategic Air Command. Change was still in the wind when the 706th was redesignated the 389th Missile Wing on July 1, 1961. The Atlas missile became an important part of the Cuban missile crisis in 1962 when the missiles were placed in launch-ready status for seven days. The last Atlas left the base by 1965.

The early 1960s saw the change from Atlas missiles on base to the Minuteman system. In 1963, the base was realigned and designated as the 90th Strategic Missile Wing (replacing the 389th) under Strategic Air Command. During World War II, the 90th Bomb Group flew over the South Pacific dropping bombs out of B-24 Liberators. Its commanding officer was Col. Arthur Rodgers. The men from this group discovered there was a pirate in the South Pacific who liked to party and whose last name was Rodgers (like their commanding officer); the pirate's his nickname was "Jolly." A decision was made by the group to adapted the skull and crossbones to a "skull and crossbombs" for their patch because of the "Rodger" name. Members of each of the four missile squadrons in the 90th Strategic Missile Wing wore a patch, which corresponded to the original World War II 90th Bomb group—the 319th, 320th, 321st, and 400th squadrons. The new Minuteman system with its solid rocket fuel was ready for launching in minutes, compared to the Atlas missile, which took over an hour to fuel in preparation for launch. In total, 200 Minuteman I missiles, located in the tri-state region of Wyoming, Nebraska, and Colorado, were controlled by base personnel.

Since the 1950s, the mission of the base has been the Atlas, Minuteman I, Minuteman III, and Peacekeeper missile systems encompassing over 12,500 square miles in Wyoming, Colorado, and Nebraska. During the Cold War, the base was known as "the most powerful installation," with over 150 Minuteman and 50 Peacekeeper missiles protecting Americans 24 hours a day, seven days a week. Thanks in part to F.E. Warren's Peacekeeper missile system, the Cold War ended without having to launch a single missile. The base has been assigned to Strategic Air Command, Air Combat Command, Space Command, and, currently, to Global Strike Command. To date, the base controls 150 Minuteman III missiles.

The historic structures still in use on base were built starting in 1885. In 1979, the facility was designated a historic site with several historic districts and over 200 structures listed in the National Register of Historic Places. There are over 26 different styles of houses found on Officers' Row, and over five different styles of homes on Sergeants' Row. The historical integrity of structures on the base has been maintained by the military.

One

Coffee, Hardtack, and Salt Pork

Army Mission and Units Assigned from 1867 to 1947

A caisson is hitched to a mule led by an unidentified soldier from D Company, 20th Infantry, on May 22, 1933. The original one-story brick barracks with covered porches are in the background. This mule was kept in excellent shape and reflects the care given to horses and mules by the Army. (WSA, Stimson.)

The primary roads from Cheyenne and the Cheyenne Depot converge at the front gate without any fencing system attached. In 1888, the post commander requested a gate be added as a speed deterrent. Two young ladies liked to race through the parade field, and the commander wanted to slow them down. (WSA.)

Unidentified troops are preparing to stand at attention on the original parade field, named Marne Parade Field in the 20th century, while the commanding officer completes a review of the troops in 1888. In the background are, from the left, the water tower, Quarters No. 1, and the first built post commander's Headquarters Building. (FEW.)

Six Army ambulances are on Argonne Parade Field; each is being pulled by a pair of horses during a military parade. This was the typical method of transportation used by the military for moving many officer families from post to post during the 1800s. (WSA.)

Shown is an unidentified cavalryman in his dress uniform standing with a black horse with a halter during the winter. Notice the excellent condition of the horse for this time of year. Horses were well cared for throughout the year because they were the military's primary mode of transportation. If the horses could not do their jobs, then neither could the military. (WSA.)

Two unidentified early-1900s soldiers are standing in front of a Sibley tent. This tent was designed by Henry Sibley in 1856 and used by the military clear into the 20th century. It stood about 12 feet high, was 18 feet in diameter, and could hold about 12 men. The men are both wearing canvas puttees (leggings) and jodhpurs. (FEW.)

Unidentified infantry officers in Spanish-American War uniforms from the late 1890s are on the steps of Headquarters Building. Officers all carried an Army-issued saber strapped on their left sides so it could readily be pulled out with their right hand when needed. High-necked wool blouses were the style of uniforms worn at that time. (WSA.)

The 9th Cavalry has gathered for a group photograph during World War I. The 9th and 10th Cavalries were designated all-black units since the Civil War and were honorably called buffalo soldiers by Indians in the 1800s. Men in white coats are cooks for the unit. (WSA.)

The train depot is located by the water tower at the post because steam engines filled up with water and coal or wood for fuel. In the foreground are the scales for weighing any freight to be picked up by the train. The offices of Wells Fargo and Company Express were located on the right of the building. (FEW.)

These unidentified mounted troops in formation are from the 9th Cavalry. In the foreground, their horses are hitched to wagons. The first two buildings on the left are finished two-story barracks. The third building from the left, which is also a barrack, is in the process of being built. At the back, the flagpole is standing in its original location; it was later moved twice more before it found

This is an artillery unit headed west from the post toward Pole Mountain Maneuvering Range. The dust created when the artillery went on the move was seen for miles. In 1932, six horses were required to pull each caisson. Some men have an easier ride than others, as some are riding on the caissons and some on horseback. At the very far left, there is a mechanized wheeled vehicle.

a permanent home. One can see the 1885 dollhouse construction to the right of the water tower. Next is the Post Hospital. On the right are a duplex, a single, and another duplex with a porch roof under construction. The last house on the right is also under construction. (WSA.)

The post is seen in the background. Between the men and the post are Crow Creek and railroad tracks. When on campaign, life was difficult. Reveille was at daybreak, breakfast at 7:00 a.m., and taps at 9:15 p.m. to end the day with lights-out. Through regular bugle calls, the Army eliminated the need for personnel to wear watches. (WSA.)

Troops from E through H of the 12th Cavalry are on the steps of the barracks located on Warren. Mascots were a common sight for units, but this organization has adopted not only a dog but also a young man, seen sitting center. In this staged photographed, the rifles are lined up in groups and the company guidon is proudly displayed. (WSA.)

Lt. Col. J.L. Torrey is on horseback in front of Post Headquarters. He was a good friend of Pres. Teddy Roosevelt and created a special unit he called "Torrey's Rough Riders," who trained after Roosevelt's Rough Riders. This was an elite unit with specialized training that was sent to Cuba during the Spanish-American War in the 1890s. (WSA.)

Some of the unidentified construction crew are standing in front of the Post Administration Building shortly after it was constructed in 1894. The Army hired many civilian contractors to help build the post along with military personnel assigned there. Life was very monotonous, and the desertion rate was quite high. (FEW.)

In December 1910, Building No. 34 was constructed as the Post Hospital, with room for 250 beds. The total cost of the building was $242,925.45. It had a coal heater, wooden floors, a slate-and-tin roof, and was approximately 41,100 square feet, not including the basement. (WSA, Stimson.)

Nine unidentified enlisted men pose with bolt-action rifles. They are wearing campaign hats, five-button wool blouses, kersey pants, ammunition belts, and brogans from the Indian War period. Brogans from the Civil War and earlier were not made with a left and right foot, but could be worn on either foot. Troops walked through water in order to shape the shoes to their feet. (WSA.)

These men are unidentified enlisted and medical staff assigned to the base's hospital around 1910. It was not until 1889 that the Military Medical Corps was created. Prior to that time, working in the hospital was punishment for soldiers. The post was one of three selected to professionally train military hospital stewards. (WSA.)

A target range was located on the northwest side of the post to practice shooting weapons. Here, the 9th Cavalry Band is practicing in 1911–1912. Targets were created from wagon rims; one such target was shaped like a man on a horse. As told, if the horse was hit, then the man had to continue practicing. (WSA.)

Here is a pair of unidentified cavalrymen on the parade field next to the barracks in the 1920s; their uniforms date to 1913. The men have all their equipment tied onto the saddle, including a bedroll for use on maneuvers. The barracks in the background date to the late 1920s. (WSA.)

Unidentified soldiers during World War I are standing on maneuvers by their pup tent, which normally did not have ends and was just canvas draped in a "V" to offer some protection for two men sleeping in the outdoors. These two have their jodhpurs rolled up, are wearing their ammunition belts, and have their rifles propped up by the tent. (FEW.)

These unidentified officers are completing maneuvers training during World War I; the Quartermaster School also included a school for officers. The camp stove was hauled out by wagon and used to cook hot meals for troops completing training. Each man was issued a mess kit. The kit consisted of fork, spoon, and knife, and the bottom and top served as skillet and plate. (WSA.)

World War I flying ace pilot Eddie Rickenbacker crashed his plane when he hit a ditch on the runway during a night-flight landing after flying 1,600 miles in 13 hours from San Francisco to Cheyenne on May 26, 1921. He landed on the only runway ever located at the installation. (FEW.)

In the 1920s, this was a common sight found at the post. Unidentified cavalry troops are completing drills on the parade field. (WSA.)

It is break time for these unidentified men resting by the combat wagon out on maneuvers in the 1920s. Water is stored in the Lister bag held up with a tripod. This bag has built-in faucets. To the right is a supply tent. (FEW.)

Brig. Gen. John Jenkins is presenting awards to the 13th Cavalry in 1924. The honor guard to the left is carrying the US and unit flags. The unidentified officers on the right are wearing winter wool coats, leather riding boots with spurs, leather gauntlets, and hold military-issued sabers. The unidentified commanding officer is wearing Army-issued jodhpurs with puttees (leggings) on his lower legs. (WSA.)

This unidentified soldier in the 1920s is pointing at the maneuver's latrine. The men dug holes in the ground and covered them with boxes, then put up tent poles with canvas draped around the area for privacy. The poles are secured with ropes to keep them upright. (FEW.)

Riding on covered wagons pulled by four-mule teams, 4th Brigade Troops are providing a Saturday morning parade review in 1927. All military harnesses were embellished with brass circles and embossed with a *US* marking the tack as military. A soldier belonged to the Army 24 hours a day, seven days a week. (WSA.)

As they did not like to walk, cavalrymen would normally be seen on horses. This is an unusual picture as these unidentified men are sitting on the porch of a barrack for a picture. The men in the front are wearing military-issued spurs, which usually did not have rowels but just a protruding arm, so a soldier could not accidently cause injury to a horse. (WSA.)

Pictured here are thousands of caissons stored on post. From 1900 to the 1930s, the mission was as a training center for the artillery. The post was designated so because of the abundance of grass and the closeness of the water supply for livestock. Normally, four to six horses would be hitched to one caisson pulling a cannon. Only one or two horses were needed to pull a machine gun. (FEW.)

Troops usually trained for maneuvers on the post. There is an unidentified man in the foreground sitting at the entrance of the double-length pup tent. Rifles are propped up together with care to keep them out of the dirt. In the background are several of the duplexes on Officers' Row. (FEW.)

The military was known to place everything in a precision line, including pup tents out on maneuvers—even if they went up and down the hill. The pup tents were just big enough for a man to crawl into and barely sit up. Canteens, rifles, and hats were propped at the doorway of the tent. These unidentified men are waking to the bugle call of reveille. (FEW.)

The Army hired civilians over the years to fill positions as needed. Initially, men were employed to help build the structures on the post; as years went by, more civilians were hired to complete all types of jobs. Typically, women were placed as secretaries. Here, Fran Dauterman is taking dictation from the Quartermaster School base commander, H.L. Whittaker. (FEW.)

In the 1930s, unidentified artillery troops are on review on Argonne Parade Field and will eventually completed the circle around the parade field in the background. Notice the troops are keeping step with the hitched mules. Both mules and horses were used by the artillery to pull machine guns loaded on caissons. (WSA.)

Unidentified soldiers are loading supplies and equipment just prior to heading out on maneuvers in 1934. Among the items still to be packed are bedrolls, which are draped over the railing of the upstairs porch. Maneuvers were 100-mile trips that were taken annually. (FEW.)

A hook and ladder truck has unidentified firemen standing on and around it in the late 1930s. Protective gear has drastically changed over the years in safeguarding first responders. The first wheeled fire vehicles were fire handcarts pulled by troops, which contained a water tank and hose. Fire destroyed over a quarter of the post in the late 1800s. (FEW.)

Unidentified soldiers are practicing precision drill marching in the 1930s on Argonne Parade Field. Each man has his legs wrapped with puttees, a bayonet scabbard attached to his ammunition belt, and is wearing a strap to keep his hat on. All are carrying their rifles on their right shoulders. The post's flagpole is in the background. (FEW.)

During the late 1930s, the front gate was open to any visitor who wanted to come to the post. The building on the right is an information center. The road leaving the post ends at the Wyoming State Capitol in downtown Cheyenne. The front gate was moved in closer to the post when Interstate 25 was built through Cheyenne and the installation. (FEW.)

The Quartermaster Training School is holding a ceremony on the field, and training center buildings are seen in the background. Unidentified troops are standing at attention on the left, and visitors are gathered along the road leading to the back gate, behind them on the right. (FEW.)

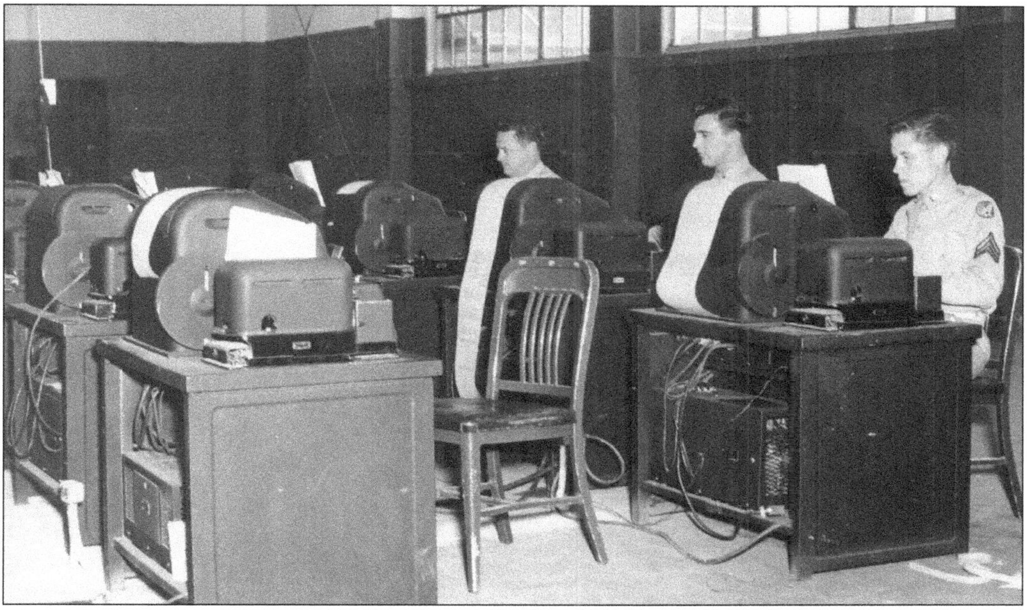

Specialty training was taught at Warren. One specialty school was Fixed Wire Communication. Here are unidentified soldiers in the 1940s at Warren, where the Quartermaster Training School was located. Other specialty schools were for construction, telegraph, secretarial, and reserve officer training. (WSA.)

Unidentified students are learning baking techniques to make bread and rolls for hundreds of people. These students are attending the Quartermaster Training School in the 1940s specifically for baker's school, which was one of many specialty schools that taught men career skills. (WSA.)

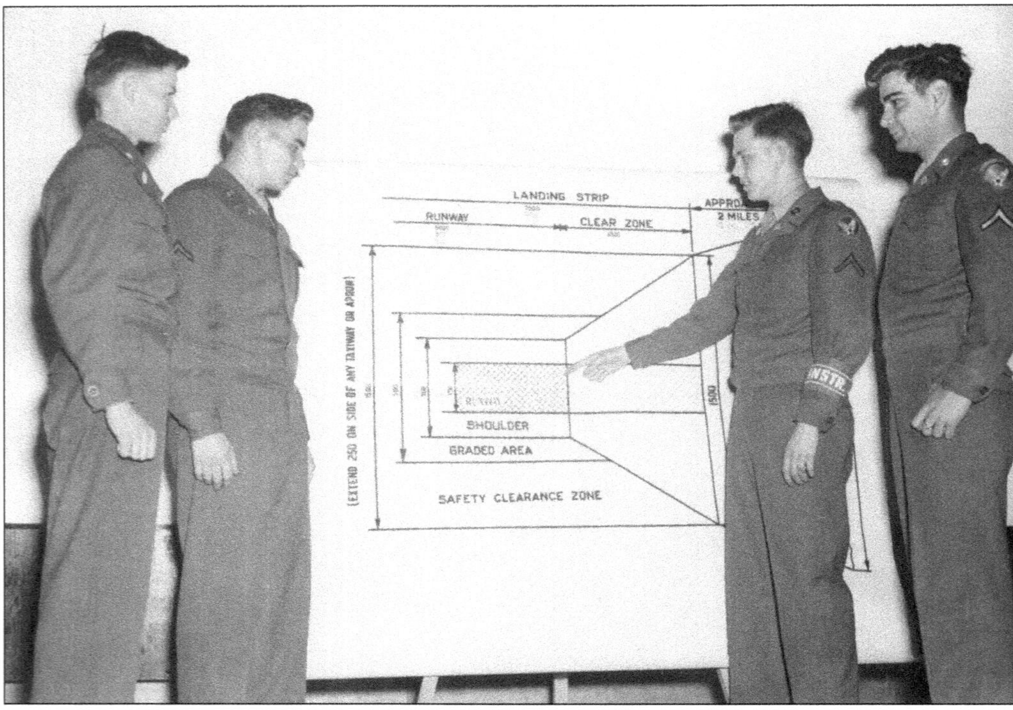

Four unidentified construction technician students are studying the building plans for an airstrip at Fort Warren in September 1948. A soldier with this kind of construction background was always needed by the military, even if Fort Warren did not have a runway. (WSA.)

Unidentified members of Class 81, graduating from the Leadership Training Branch of the Training Division, pose on the grass outside one of the Quartermaster Training buildings during the 1940s. Most of these enlisted men have insignias on their collars and have their earned ranks on their sleeves. (FEW.)

This is the Training Cadre, Company D of the Second Quartermaster Training School in front of one of the school's buildings. Within six months, 282 buildings were constructed to house a garrison of 20,000 soldiers. It took 5,000 men from Wyoming to build it. This made two commands at the post. Post Headquarters was on one side of Crow Creek, and the Quartermaster Replacement Training Center on the other. (FEW.)

One of the jobs assigned to a soldier living in the barracks in the Quartermaster Training Center was to load coal into the stoker and remove the burnt coal "clinkers" to keep it running in the winter. If a soldier fell asleep during night duty on the furnace, the whole barracks would punish that member. The man holding the shovel is unidentified. (FEW.)

Unidentified troops learned to type on manual typewriters at Quartermaster Training School during the 1940s. Unlike a computer keyboard, a manual typewriter's keys had to be struck by each finger with a strong downstroke. Most people would have problems using their little fingers properly. (WSA.)

Unidentified men are holding rifles in front of the Quartermaster Training School barracks in the 1940s. All are in high-top lace-up shoes, which provided some protection for their ankles from sprains when marching. They are also wearing fatigue caps, which mimicked Navy-style hats. (FEW.)

Here, in preparation for World War II combat, four unidentified soldiers practice crawling in dugout trenches and shooting from foxholes. Men became accustomed to carrying multiple pouches on their cartridge belts to hold ammunition for their Winchester Model 1917 bolt-action .30-06 rifles. This was a World War I firearm that was reworked for World War II. Taking care of one's weapon was another task required by the Army. (FEW.)

Unidentified soldiers from the Signal Corps train during World War II by climbing a wall with ropes, while hauling their bedrolls, canteen, ammunition, rifle, and other equipment. (WSA.)

As a military vehicle, jeeps became commonly used during World War II. They were versatile and were the primary mode of transportation for officers during the war. Unidentified men are sitting in this jeep with a convertible top, windshield, four-wheel drive, and no doors. (FEW.)

In the foreground is a 1940s soldier "walking guard" in front of the wooden chapel, built during World War II. This was a common duty given to men who had been in trouble. Most soldiers ended up pulling guard duty at some point in their early careers. (FEW.)

During World War II, unidentified men are marching in precision step. They are wearing leggings, fatigue uniforms, and ammunition belts. Each soldier is carrying his rifle on his right shoulder. The military prides itself on its precision formations when marching. (FEW.)

Pictured during the 1940s, this recently fired cannon shows muzzle flash shooting from the end of the cannon barrel. An unidentified soldier has just pulled the lanyard. Only trained men fired the weapons, as safety was always an issue. The cannon was usually pulled behind a caisson. Buildings on the post are in the background. (FEW.)

An armored six-wheeled vehicle with two unidentified men resting on the front is parked next to one of the barrack buildings located on post. On the top of the vehicle is a spotlight, and the two windows are protected with drop window guards. (FEW.)

While on maneuvers, this unidentified soldier is riding on an official Army motorcycle. The man is wearing a football helmet. This was probably a typical piece of safety equipment worn before military helmets were required. An armored six-wheeled vehicle is seen in the background. (FEW.)

Pictured is the backside aerial view of the hospital complex in the 1940s and 1950s. Additional hospital wards were created from wooden barracks in the foreground. The large three-story brick building directly behind the wooden wards was constructed as a dormitory. Building No. 34, the primary hospital structure, was the largest edifice in the complex and was located just behind the brick dormitory. (FEW.)

An unidentified soldier is standing next to his personal motorcycle with a 1945 Wyoming license plate. He is wearing camouflage coveralls, snow boots, and gloves to help keep warm in the winter snow. He is just outside the barracks in the courtyard. On the brick wall are the remnants of the removed balcony porch. (FEW.)

On January 2, 1949, a 100-year storm hit southeastern Wyoming and lasted for three days, with wind blowing 75 miles an hour. This was the worst storm on record, killing numerous people and thousands of livestock. The military came to the aid of ranchers by dropping hay from airplanes, which was named Operation Haylift. Three unidentified troopers are here with a converted truck used as a snowplow. (FEW.)

Two

Sentinels in the Rockies

Air Force Mission and Units Assigned from 1947 to 2005

Here is a view of the front gate taken in February 1956 after a snowstorm. The name was officially changed to Francis E. Warren Air Force Base from Fort Warren in 1949, two years after being designated an Air Force base. An unidentified soldier is standing in the entrance in his winter wool uniform coat and "wheel" dress hat. (FEW.)

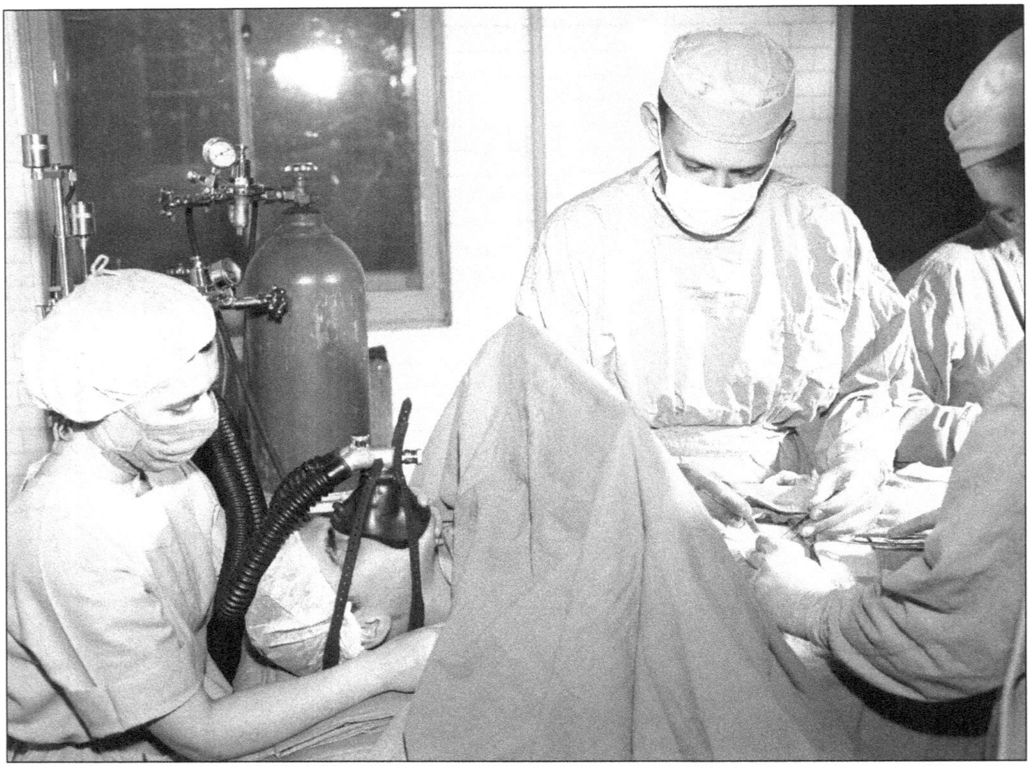

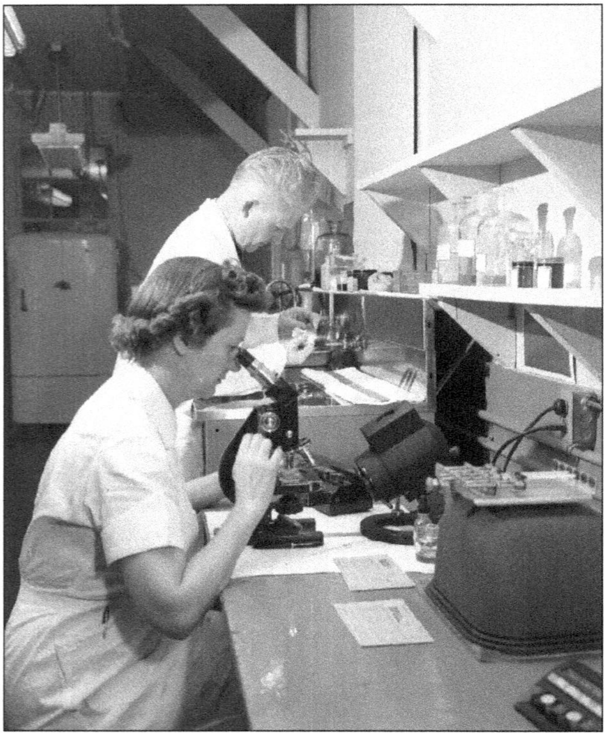

In 1958, the hospital operating room was on the third floor of Building No. 34. The hospital did not have elevators, and patients had to be carried up and down the stairs for surgery. Eventually, several elevators were installed to make life easier. Pictured are an unidentified surgery team and patient. (FEW.)

Rheumatic fever and strep throat were common in the Rocky Mountain region. Prior to the creation and use of antibiotics, many people died because of these illnesses. In the 1950s, the base was chosen to participate in a study to determine the cause of strep throat. Here, unidentified personnel are part of the study, which found that a streptococcus bacteria caused the sickness. (FEW.)

Modern pharmacy technicians have the aid of mechanized pill dispensers, but these men in April 1958 are filling prescriptions by hand. One requirement that has not changed from then to now is the white uniform. Also, these men are both sporting the "James Dean" hairstyle of the 1950s. (FEW.)

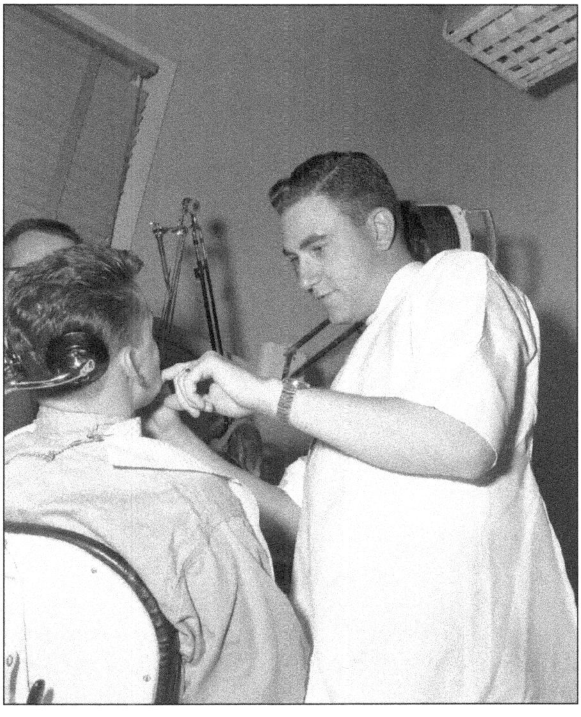

An unidentified dental technician and dentist are working on an unidentified soldier on May 8, 1958. Most dental hand tools have not really changed over the years. With free dental and medical care, men are always kept in good physical condition by the military. (FEW.)

Preparing grilled sandwiches for hungry airmen in June 1964 are, from left to right, SSgt. James Morgan, assistant mess sergeant; SSgt. Lionel LeClair, shift leader; and SSgt. Nick Scorcio, first cook. New buffet lines were added to the two base dining halls' noon food service. Airmen in a hurry chose the buffet line for short-order sandwiches, soup, salads, and cold plates rather than the regular complete hot plate service. (WSA.)

From 1947 to 1958, the mission of the base was a training school for the newly formed Air Force. This school trained airmen in their career fields. After completing other military requirements, these men, with military-style haircuts and military-issued eyeglasses, attend classes in their uniforms. (FEW.)

Four unidentified soldiers are preparing for the day while shaving using a mirror hung on a pine tree in 1958. All are using safety razors and shaving cream to accomplish their tasks. Instead of their fatigue uniform, all four men seem to be wearing coveralls. Also in the area are several aspen trees (FEW.)

Unidentified men are standing by aspen trees waiting to eat while on a training mission at Pole Mountain. The lieutenant on the right has his mess kit hanging ready from his fingers. Several others are carrying their canteens from their belts. The soldiers carried their own mess kits and were responsible for keeping their own utensils clean. (FEW.)

This unidentified female soldier is a member of the technical school's 3452th Student Squadron Women in the Air Force, or WAF, in May 1958. She holds the rank of airman and wears one stripe on her sleeve. Women had a unique hat with the Air Force's insignia on the front; women in the military today are still allowed to wear skirts. (FEW.)

During the 1950s, the Air Force public affairs office broadcast a radio station with call letters WFW. Two unidentified soldiers are working in the booth. The military published a newspaper, called the *Sentinel*, which is still published weekly. Over the years, the military also had a television station. (FEW.)

The Atlas missile was the first American intercontinental missile, and F.E. Warren Air Force Base had 24 located in Wyoming, Colorado, and Nebraska. This missile was powered by a highly combustible fuel that was only mixed for use when the missile was prepared for launch. The missile was deployed at the base from 1958 to the mid-1960s. (FEW.)

The 706th Strategic Missile Wing's three squadrons—the 549th, 564th, and the 565th—had the honor of posturing the first Atlas D missiles. The Atlas was a liquid-fuel missile housed in a coffin-like launch facility and stored horizontally until launching. The gantry held the rocket upright. When commanded, an Atlas could be refueled and launched in one hour. (WSA.)

A model of the Atlas missile is displayed on the left in this photograph. The military band is seated during the official ceremony in which the base was designated as the first operational missile base in the Air Force on June 10, 1958. This was the beginning of the new mission for the base in which the troops were all assigned to Strategic Air Command. (FEW.)

From 1958 to 1963, the mission of the base was the Atlas intercontinental ballistic missile system, the missile that protected America during the beginning of the Cold War. This tractor-trailer carries a missile onto the prairies, where launch facilities were located in a three-state region. (FEW.)

Capt. Jerome L. Newton, seated, and Capt. Thompson R. Foster, standing, are the officers on the last crew to pull alert duty at the 564th site for an Atlas missile in October 1964. The Atlas launching consoles were different from the Minuteman system consoles. Crew members wore white one-piece uniforms for safety. If a uniform showed possible signs of a fuel spill, the crewman was removed from the site. (WSA.)

A Minuteman I transporter erector is upright so that a Minuteman I can be lowered into the launch facility. Eventually, the base was responsible for 200 Minuteman I B model missiles, which were three-stage solid-propellant rockets with a range of 5,500 nautical miles and improved accuracy over their predecessor. They cost $7 million each. (FEW.)

On June 12, 1964, Warren reached a milestone "on-alert" status of Minuteman intercontinental ballistic missiles. The day marked an end of construction of 200 silo launch facilities and 20 launch control centers. The passing of the key from the contractor to military personnel was the symbolic end of construction. From left to right are William Scheizer, William McMurrain, Lt. Col. Willard Norris, Col. William E. Todd, and Robert Randall. (WSA.)

Presenting the official Minuteman I Squadron commander's hard hat for wear in the field is Col. F.E. Wilkstrom (left), commander of the 90th Strategic Missile Wing, who congratulates Col. James M. Bagley, named squadron commander of the 400th Strategic Missile Squadron, at formal activation ceremonies. The 400th joined three other 90th Minuteman I squadrons at a ceremony on July 1, 1964, one year after the wing was activated. (WSA.)

The terrain around the base was ideal for solid rocket-fueled missiles. This northern-latitude location was sparsely populated and far enough inland to preclude an attack from sea-launched ballistic missiles. Warren became the first operational Minuteman I missile base in the Air Force in March 1963. Pictured are unidentified Boeing personnel preparing a reentry vehicle on a Minuteman I missile for a test. (FEW.)

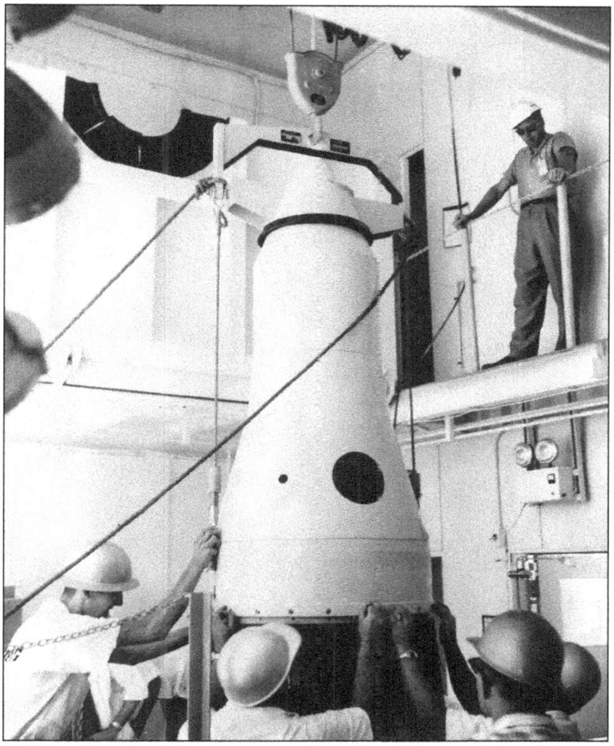

With a law enforcement escort for security, the Minuteman I missile transporter-erector vehicle transports the weapon. This transporter-erector was the first to arrive on base for a test drive around the base in January 1964. It measures over 63 feet long and tips the scales at nearly 108,000 pounds when carrying a Minuteman I to each of the 200 silo launch facilities surrounding the base. (WSA.)

In 1965, the day begins for Captain Bourgeois (left) and Captain Marks, both members of the 319th Strategic Missile Squadron, preparing to depart to the missile field. The missileers, crewmen responsible for monitoring and launching the missile, wear one-piece white "bags" uniforms and red leather hats with white lettering. (WSA.)

The commander along with the other officers whose duty it was to monitor and launch the Minuteman I missile arrived for predeparture briefing each morning. Officers were informed as to situations before driving to the field. (WSA.)

Teams of two missileers are assigned, with one man as commander of the crew and the other as deputy. Each crew member has his own classified lock that has to be retrieved prior to "tripping out" to the missile field for 30 hours of work. Captain Bourgeois (left) and Captain Marks (right) are retrieving their assigned locks in 1965. (WSA.)

The missile field—12,500 square miles in Wyoming, Colorado, and Nebraska—had 200 Minuteman I missiles monitored by crews 24 hours a day, 365 days a year. Here, missileers have driven to the missile field as Captain Marks opens the guarded gate at the missile-alert facility, where the communication equipment for monitoring the missile was located. Sites are 40–125 miles away from the base. (WSA.)

Once the crew arrives at the missile site, weapons are issued in the flight security control center by air policeman A1C Tom Barbetta (right) to Captain Marks (left) and Captain Bougeois (center), members of the 319th Strategic Missile Squadron, in 1965. Present-day missileers are no longer issued weapons to carry. (WSA.)

Missileers work underground. The only way to enter the capsule is through an elevator that takes the crews seven stories underground. Taking the elevator down to the office are Captain Bougeois (left) and Captain Marks, who will work for 30 hours before returning to the base. (WSA.)

A smiling welcome is shared by relieved crew member 1st Lt. H.C. Schenkenberger (left) with Captain Bougeois (center) and Captain Marks in 1965. Schenkenberger is pushing open the blast door, which will be closed when Bougeois and Marks clear for entrance and Schenkenberger and the other team member leave. The door is locked and left until the next team arrives to take over from Bougeois and Marks. (WSA.)

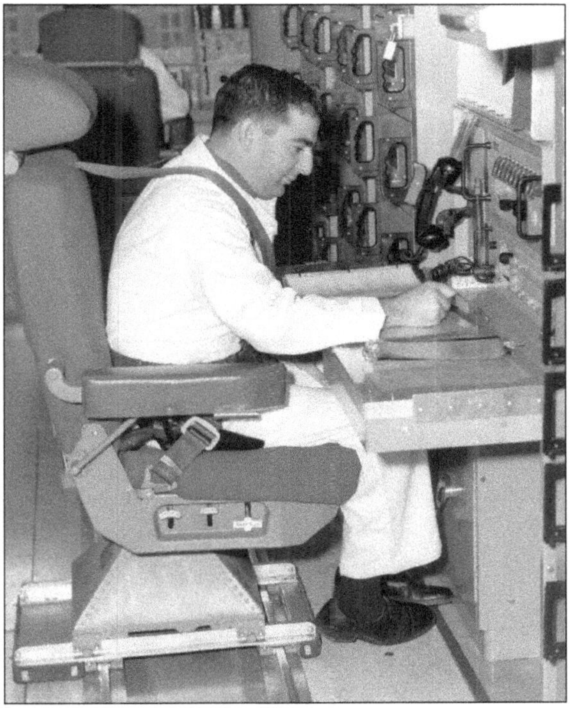

319th Strategic Missile Squadron crew members work a 30-hour alert, monitoring the missile communication equipment and preparing to launch a Minuteman I missile if directed by the president of the United States. Each crew member knows how the equipment works. Captain Marks is sitting in a strapped chair in case of possible earthquakes or incoming missiles so the missile can be launched in reciprocation if needed. (WSA.)

Missileers 1st Lt. Carl I. Peterson (sitting) and Capt. Eric C. Peterson change out paper on communication equipment during an evaluation on November 22, 1977. These men are in charge of monitoring the missiles and launching them against enemies when official messages are received. The men are wearing two-piece blue cotton uniforms. (FEW.)

During their off time from "tripping out" to the field, soldiers train to pull a 24-hour shift monitoring the communication equipment of the missile systems. 1st Lt. Carl I. Peterson and Capt. Eric C. Peterson depart from the missile procedures trainer after an evaluation on November 22, 1977. On Captain Peterson's left pocket is what missileers refer to as a "pocket rocket." This is a badge worn by officially trained missileers. (FEW.)

Presently, three missiles are at the front gate. Shown is the installation of the Minuteman I, the first one placed on exhibit in June 1964 and, in 2012, the smallest one closest to the modern helicopter. The three men on the cherry picker are from civil engineering on base and are Albert Prall, Elisha Page, and Art VanPelt; they bolted together the two sections of the 55-foot static display. (WSA.)

The 90th Security Police Group is receiving the Gen. Curtis E. LeMay Trophy for being the "Best Security Police Unit in the Strategic Air Command, 1980." Lt. Gen. James F. Mullins (left), the Fifteenth Air Force commander, presented the trophy to Col. Larry B. Hughes, 90th Security Police Group commander in April 24, 1981. (FEW.)

Some of base's hardware is on display at the Cheyenne Airport during Armed Forces Day, May 16, 1981. Pictured are, from left to right, a transporter-erector, a payload transportation van, and a van. All were used to take missile components and related equipment to the missile site areas. (FEW.)

Colonel Wilkstrom (right) receives a plaque signifying the completion of the site activation activities in the Warren Air Force Base area from Col. William E. Todd on June 30, 1965. Most of the other missile bases had only 150 missiles, so the base was proud to have manned 200 missiles. (FEW.)

Pictured is a series compiled by the original photographer showing a Minuteman III missile launch from Vandenberg Air Force Base, California. The Minuteman III missile, using solid rocket fuel, is ready to be launched in a minute's notice. Warren at one time had 200 Minuteman IIIs, but the number has been decreased to 150 missiles. They have been located on the base since 1963. (FEW.)

Pictured is a typical launch center where unidentified Minuteman III missileers pulled alerts while stationed. These centers were cramped, allowed no privacy, and had few comforts for the combat crew member on alert. The area offered a prison toilet and sink. Although some of the equipment has been updated; the space has not changed, with the exception that crews are mixed men and women at present. (FEW.)

Sgt. Matthew Bounds (left) and SSgt. Barry Williams, one of the 90th's electronic lab teams, perform power-up procedures on April 12, 1991. The two are wearing battle dress uniforms, commonly known by soldiers as BDUs. These men earned $800 per month when they first joined the military in the mid-1980s (FEW.)

Periodically, the launcher closure door must be refurbished by maintenance personnel. Unidentified workers roll the door back, clean it, and remove corrosion on all surfaces including the bearing surface and debris bins. The bearing surface is re-beveled if necessary, and the door is painted and sealed to inhibit corrosion. This work was completed in 1980. (FEW.)

An unidentified member of the 90th Maintenance Group in a safety cage has lowered himself alongside to complete maintenance on a Minuteman III missile in 1980. This is the approved method of repairing a missile while it is installed in the launch facility. (FEW.)

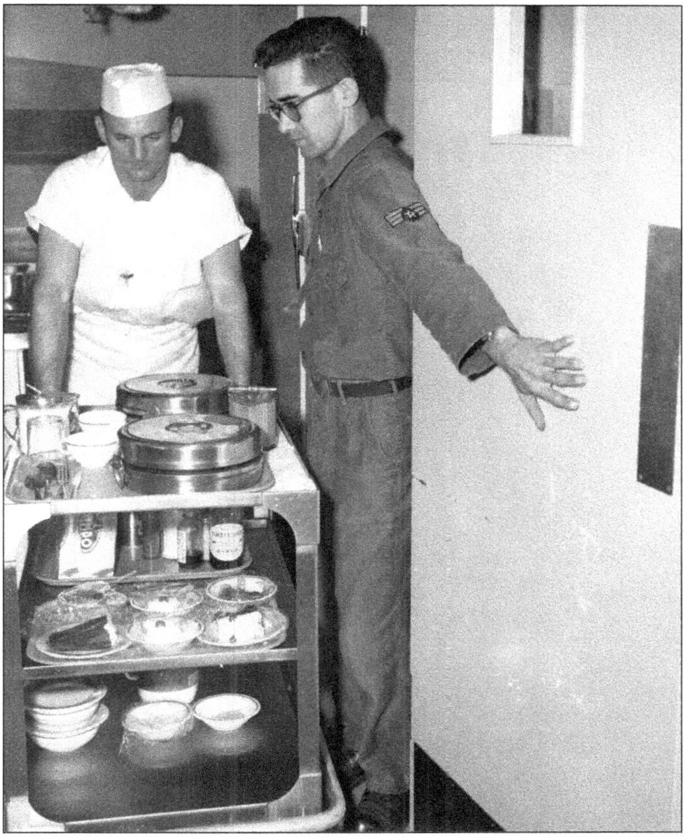

A2C Frantz, missile site cook, brings food to the crew pulling an alert in the Launch Control Center. The site manager has opened the door for the cook. Each launch control center has a site manager who is responsible for checking in all personnel, any maintenance that might be needed on the site, and all structures. (FEW.)

An unidentified enlisted man (left) serves fried chicken to Col. John Gordon, 90th Strategic Missile Wing commander, during the mobility/deployment portion of an inspection from December 5 through 15, 1988. The base completes multiple inspections to make sure that everyone does his or her job properly so that the nuclear mission is completed without mistakes. (FEW.)

On April 5, 1991, 90th Strategic Missile Wing maintenance personnel perform a bonding check topside from the training facility located on base. SSgt Mark Allison (squatting on the right) is evaluating troops. From left to right are SSgt. Joe Burnett, Robert Gregory, Russell Kemp, and SrA. Harold Plitt. Safety equipment is always used by base personnel when working on the missiles. (FEW.)

Unidentified members of F.E. Warren's 90th Security Police Group board an Air Force KC-135 plane to begin the long and arduous journey to Saudi Arabia in support of Operation Desert Shield in June 1990. Troops, dressed in "chocolate chip" uniforms, are carrying all their belongings and weapons for the trip. (FEW.)

A1C Janice M. Ethier, from the 90th Transportation Squadron, is trying out a new compact truck, one of eight received in 1979. Missileers, maintenance personnel, and security forces personnel drove thousands of miles. Keeping vehicles in top shape was a hard task for the 90th Transportation Squadron troops. (FEW.)

The Peacekeeper was deployed only at F.E. Warren Air Force Base, and the base had 50 located on the prairies in Wyoming. This is a cold-launch missile, which utilizes steam to lift the missile out of the ground prior to the engines firing, and it is capable of multiple warheads. Each one cost $70 million. This missile was deployed at the base from 1988 to 2005. (FEW.)

A Peacekeeper stage III container is being moved into an Emplacer vehicle for moving in the fall of 1988. Fifty Peacekeeper missiles were deployed to Wyoming and placed in converted Minuteman III launch facilities. F.E. Warren was the only base with Peacekeeper missiles, and the system was deactivated in 2005. The missile could not be transported as a whole, so it was moved in stages with specialized vehicles. (FEW.)

A vehicle called the Emplacer was used to help lower the different stages of the Peacekeeper. Peacekeeper stage I is transferred by rolling it into the Emplacer on May 16, 1986. This missile was larger than the Minuteman system and so could not be lowered into the launch facility as a whole, but in sections. (FEW.)

Unidentified members of the 90th Security Police Group are sitting inside a KC-135 traveling to Saudi Arabia in support of Operation Desert Shield in June 1990. Most of the troops sent to the war zone were security police, but members of the 90th Civil Engineers Squadron also deployed to build any required structures. (FEW.)

A1C Ronnie Powell is monitoring radio transmissions while keeping an eye on vehicles approaching the main gate, Gate No. 1, in 1991. In 1971, Francis E. Warren Air Force Base's A1C Kathleen Enderson was Strategic Air Command's first female security policeperson. Security police traditionally made up the largest group, with over 1,200 soldiers assigned, with a mean age of 23. (FEW.)

The middle female soldier in this unidentified mobility team is hospital spokesperson Airman First Class Morrison. She ensures security members have met medical requirements for deployment during a mobility exercise in 1991. This is the way the military verified that troops were ready to be deployed. (FEW.)

Three

High-Class Living, or Not

Officers' Row, Sergeants' Row, and Administrative Buildings

This building, the first permanent hospital, replaced the original hospital. With 6,200 square feet, not including the basement, it was built in 1887 at the cost of $13,903. In June 1928, the structure was remodeled, at the cost of $8,243, to house 11 noncommissioned officers' families. Nine apartments were on the first floor, with two apartments on the second floor. (WSA)

Building No. 210 was constructed as the Post Administration Building in 1894 and was originally Building No. 38. It cost $8,604. It has wooden floors, a slate roof, and 2,858 square feet. The second floor was used as an open functional activity room for military ceremonies, post dances, church, and theatrical productions. (FEW.)

This building was erected to house 127 men who worked in the hospital in 1908. The post commander decided the building was too nice to be used for barracks and decided to change the building into Post Headquarters for his office space. In 1928, remodeling began on the second floor for the Officer's Club. (FEW.)

On the left is a building used as Company Headquarters, and placed next to it is one of the two-story barracks. In the background are a fire station, blacksmith shop, and horse stable. Also in the distant background are unidentified people walking and riding a horse. (FEW.)

Blacksmith shops and fire stations were spaced in between the barracks and stables. Built in 1908 at the cost of $2,674 with 750 square feet, this blacksmith shop was typical. Later on, the building was used as a storehouse. These buildings were only large enough to have a complete shop for one blacksmith. (FEW.)

The horse head adorning the barn door designates this building as the post's veterinary hospital. This was one of the most important buildings located on the post because if the horses were not in good condition, no one was able to go anywhere. Its 6,197 square feet was built for $25,184.75 to stall 41 animals. The left-side room had a natural skylight for operating on the horses. (FEW.)

Building No. 320 was completed in November 1909 at the cost of $15,034.89. The stable was built to keep 78 animals and had 12,233 square feet. The upstairs is a loft for storage of hay, and near the roof above the double doors is a pulley system to lift hay more easily to the loft. On the side of the building are exterior stable doors and wooden corrals for horses and mules. (WSA.)

The Riding Hall was built especially to exercise Army horses year-round to keep them in top physical shape. With 28,000 square feet, the hall was built in 1907 at the cost of $54,836. Later, the building was converted to the Base Commissary or grocery store until the 1980s, when the hall was changed into a troop exercise facility. (FEW.)

This building, known today as Fall Hall, was constructed as a gymnasium and was completed on June 15, 1940, at the cost of $207,372.88. It had 26,484 square feet, not counting the basement. The building capacity was 1,500 people. It was named after Col. Gerald G. Fall Jr., who was known to support troops. (FEW.)

Building No. 208 was constructed when the earlier barracks burned down in 1931. It cost $39,775.96 and had 7,070 square feet, not including a basement. The barracks housed 49 men and was used for the band. Because band members were not armed with weapons, the attic had gymnasium equipment installed to help the soldiers stay in shape. (WSA.)

When this 1,329-square-foot barbershop, built in 1907 for $6,587, became the Paymaster Building, window bars were installed. The far right building housed the hired gunmen awaiting trial after the Johnson County, Wyoming, cattlemen's war in 1892. The accused men were released without trial by the military as Wyoming courts could not determine where to hold the trial or who was financially responsible for the men. (WSA.)

Each company assigned to the post had its own guardhouse. Building No. 234 was completed on March 5, 1911, at the cost of $21,783 and with 4,060 square feet. The foundation is of stone and concrete, and the guardhouse has a slate roof and concrete floors. The building was a combined office and prison for soldiers. The prison part of the building could hold 19 people. (FEW.)

The Sentry Lodge was just inside the front gate on the south side of the road. The 156-square-foot building was constructed in June 1933 for $700. This was used as an information office in the 1940s before being devoted to security. The building did have a restroom, and the sink was replaced on February 3, 1937. (FEW.)

There is a car driving past the post's flagpole. The park around the flagpole is edged with white poles and painted-black metal poles. Trees and shrubs are planted around the flagpole. In the background on the left are unmarried officers' quarters and a single officers' quarters on Officers' Row. (FEW.)

This is a February 1958 view of a woodworking shop with signs posted for cleanliness and safety rules while using the equipment. At the back of the room is an area designated for smoking, as there are signs posted for no smoking around the equipment. (FEW.)

The post's wooden water tower sits between Officers' Quarters No. 1, a dollhouse, and the original wooden one-story barracks. It was several stories tall to help give water pressure for use by the post. Just behind the tower is another storage tank for water. (FEW.)

Fire was the leading disaster for an Army post, so the Army placed fire stations behind the barracks and in front of the stables. A fire station could be easily identified as there was a tower on the building. This station was built in 1909 at the cost of $3,194.63 and has 966 square feet. (FEW.)

The Red Cross received permission to construct a building on the base. The structure was used from the 1940s to the 1990s. The office trained many volunteers over the years in classes such as resuscitation. During the 1990s, the Red Cross office was moved off base, and the building was sold and moved to Laramie, Wyoming. (FEW.)

This building, presently named the Pronghorn Center, was constructed as a service club with a full basement. It featured a stage, dance floor, and pool tables for airmen to enjoy in their off time. (FEW.)

This building was constructed in the late 1940s as the Officer's Club. The prior location of the club had been in the Headquarters Building, Building No. 65, on the second floor. This picture was taken on February 20, 1958. During the 1990s, the floor in the kitchen gave out, and the building was condemned and torn down. (FEW.)

The construction of unmarried bachelor quarters, Building No. 129, was started on May 5, 1910, at the cost of $44,936.24. This building was erected to house 10 officers and had wooden floors, a tiled roof, and 11,665 square feet, not including the basement. In 1933, the heater was converted from coal to gas at the cost of $223.51. Notice the horse tied to a streetlamp. (WSA.)

These original infantry barracks, built in 1885, had space for 65 men and cost $15,902.68. The barracks had 10,092 square feet. This structure was changed to a salvage warehouse on January 5, 1926. It originally had a stone foundation, wooden shingles, and wooden floors. (FEW.)

There were actually three different styles of barracks built from 1900 to 1930. The building shown here was completed in September 14, 1908, at the cost of $91,970.48. The structure was built with a slate roof and yellow pine floors, and had 25,984 square feet. The upper floor had an open bay and housed 240 men. In May 1937, 12 lavatories were replaced at the cost of $154.20. Attics were used as firing ranges during World War II. (FEW.)

A decision was made in the late 1950s to tear down the barracks from the Quartermaster Replacement Center as the buildings were declared unfit for use. They were sold off, torn down, or even moved. One such building was purchased and became a barn for hogs north of Carpenter, Wyoming. (FEW.)

These barracks were built on the site of the buildings of the Quartermaster Training Center, which were torn down in the 1950s. The brick barracks replaced the wooden structures, were better built, and could easily house several hundred soldiers. All the barracks have gone through many different stages of remodeling, and none look like they did when originally built. (FEW.)

The original 1880s barracks were shaped in a "U." A fire destroyed the far side, and another barracks, Building No. 208, replaced it in 1930. Running along the center of the picture is the railroad with a stone-constructed storage building. More storage buildings and horse stables are in the background. Across the railroad tracks in the background is Crow Creek. (FEW.)

This northwesterly aerial view, taken between 1940 and 1960, shows Cheyenne in the lower right and predates Interstate 25, which runs north and south between the base and the city. The first oval to the left of the main road on the base is the Warren Bowl, where the military and local high schools play football. In the upper middle is the original base parade field, today named Marne Parade Field. (WSA.)

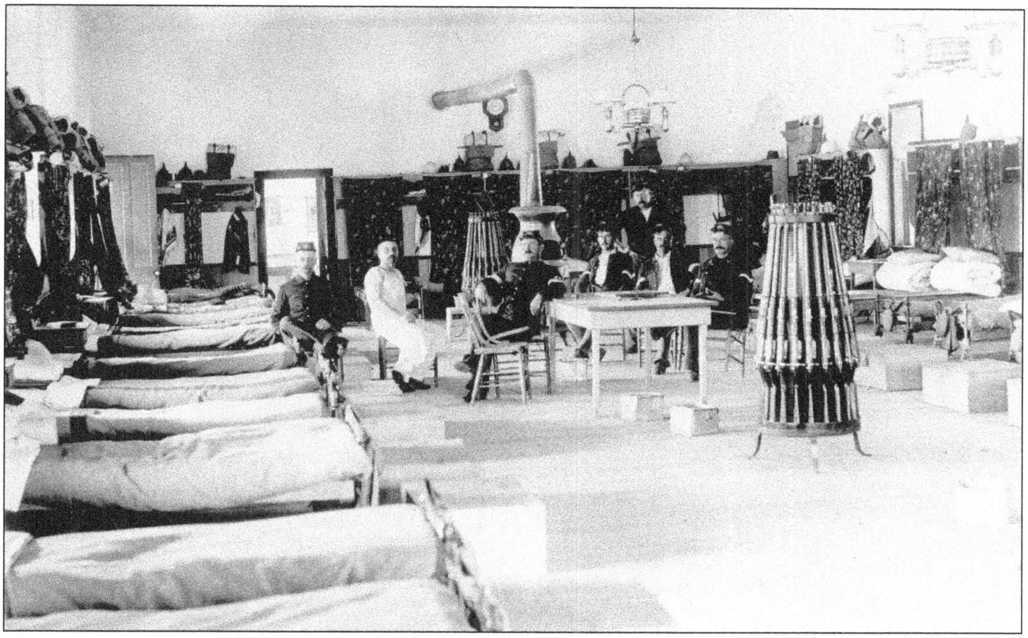

The interior of barracks Nos. 207 through 218, built after 1885, were quite simple. Helmets were stored on the tops of closets, while footlockers were kept at the ends of soldiers' beds. There were gun racks for storing rifles and gas lights hanging from the ceiling. Closets had curtain doors. The barracks were heated with "cannon heaters," which were potbelly stoves. (WSA.)

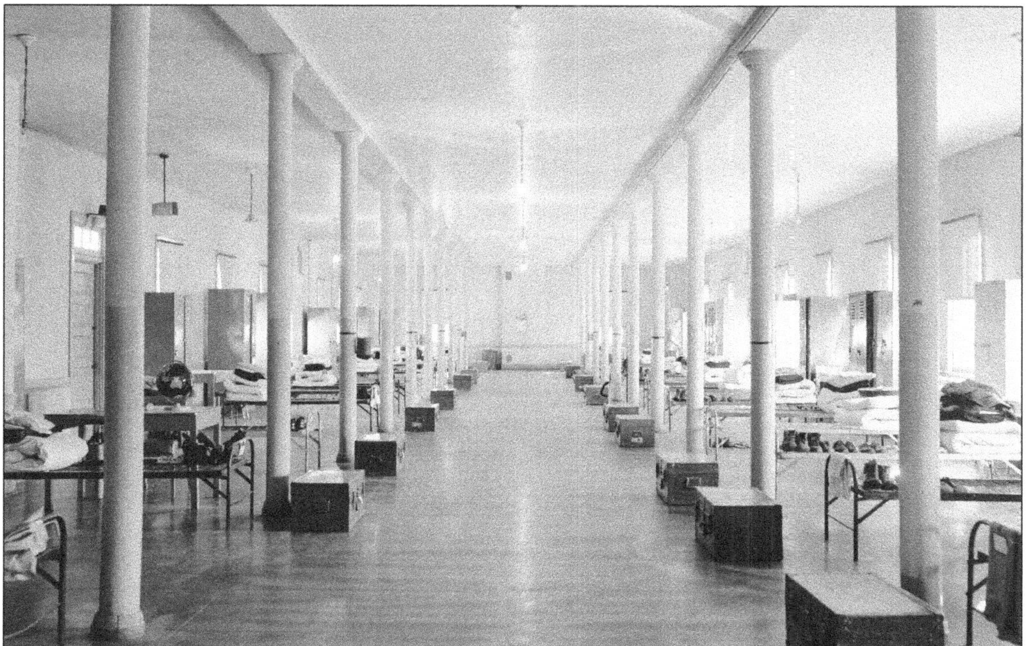

This is an interior view of an open-bay two-story barrack on May 10, 1958. Metal beds are lined up in rows, with individual footlockers at the end of the beds. Men would share the metal lockers placed between the beds for the rest of their belongings. (FEW.)

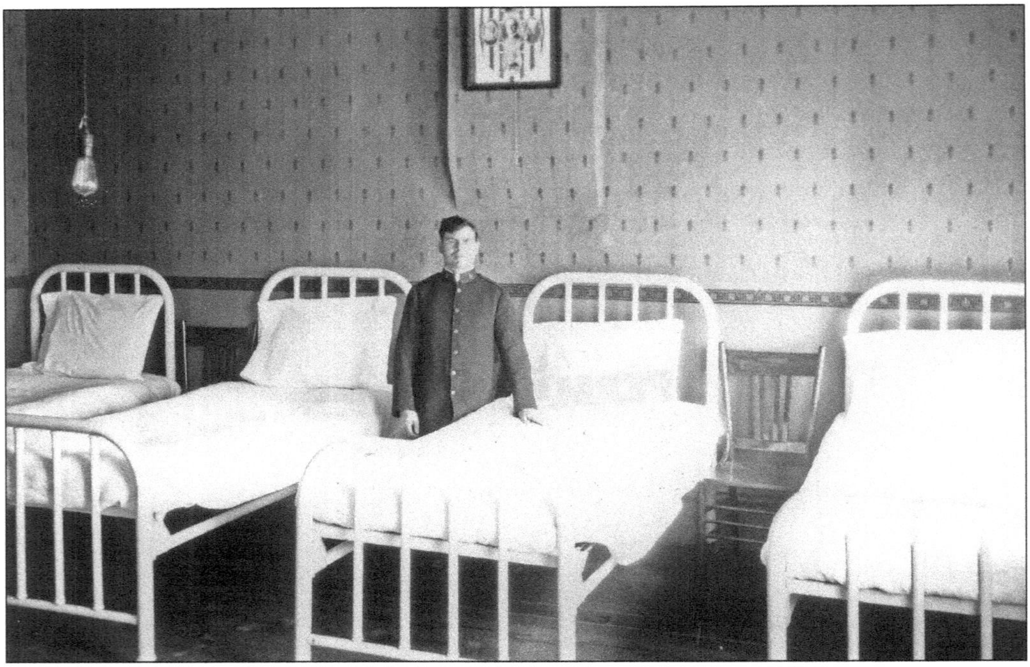

Here, a multiperson hospital ward at the post has four beds separated by wooden chairs. Notice the lack of a light fixture, with just a hanging lightbulb. The ward is decorated with wallpaper to cheer patients. The unidentified soldier is wearing the "S" insignia designating a trained hospital steward. (WSA.)

Taken in August 20, 1935, this aerial view is of the city of Cheyenne in the foreground and the post in the background. The oval circle just in front of the buildings is the Warren Bowl Stadium, built in October 1931 at the cost of $5,325, donated by the citizens of Cheyenne and the post's recreation funds. It could seat 4,157 people. (FEW.)

Along Randall Boulevard are the 1900-to-1930 two-storied barracks. These beautiful, old, stately barracks have been kept modern on the inside and historically accurate on the outside. Enlisted personnel continue to live in the structures. This postcard photograph was taken sometime between 1930 and 1949. (FEW.)

The original Officers' Row was built in 1867–1868. These quarters were wooden structures, and none survived to modern times. The post was designated a permanent post in 1884, and these buildings were gradually replaced, starting in 1885, with brick structures. (WSA.)

Pictured in 1894 are barracks numbered 212 to 216. Each cost $15,902.68 to build. The Army always constructed barracks first, prior to building quarters for officers at a fort. In 1867, the first barracks were wooden; starting in 1885, those were torn down and replaced with brick structures. Sparse in this part of Wyoming, trees were an important addition by the Army and were planted as soon as buildings were completed. (WSA.)

The oldest on the installation, seven original dollhouse quarters were built in 1885. The buildings are 2,822 square feet with shingled roofs and wooden floors. Each has a formal parlor, formal dining room, family parlor, with three bedrooms for the family, and a servant's room or extra family bedroom on the second floor. (FEW.)

With 922 square feet, this structure was originally built for a noncommissioned officer's family in 1885. Constructed at a cost of $1,200, the building has a shingled roof and a wooden floor. The porch in the back of the house was enclosed in 1928. (FEW.)

This is the view along Officers' Row. Notice the cottonwoods planted in the 1930s. The duplex is the most common type of house located on the post. There are eight styles of two-family quarters, totaling 38. Each family's side averages around 5,600 square feet. (WSA, Stimson.)

This is a backside view of original quarters, which were built in the 1800s. Quarters had garages built in the 1940s. Each structure was wired for telephones and used the quarter's number as the original phone number. Electricity was run on poles in the back of the buildings. Quarters No. 1 is the first one in the lower right-hand corner. (FEW.)

One of the early officers' duplexes, Quarters Nos. 19 and 20 was later renumbered No. 20 A and B when odd numbers were removed from the numbering system. With 5,490 total square feet on both sides, the housing was built in 1900 for $10,366.50. The quarters had three bedrooms on the second floor and two fireplaces, located in the parlor and dining room on the first floor. (FEW.)

There were seven wooden chapels built during the Quartermaster Training School of World War II. After the closure of the training school, all but one were moved off base or torn down. Several of these chapel buildings can be seen in Cheyenne and are still used for church services. (FEW.)

The Post Cemetery's white marble tombstones, provided by the US Army Quartermaster Department, face west. Started in 1867, when the post began, the cemetery was closed in 1979 by Strategic Air Command, which took reservations for the remaining plots. Buried next to the cemetery are World War II prisoners— eight Germans and one Italian—from the post's days as a prisoner-of-war camp with over 900 incarcerated. (WSA.)

The car is parked in front of the War Department Theater, which held up to 898 men. Completed on April 15, 1939, it had 10,428 square feet and cost $135,594.80. The theater faces Fall Hall, the gymnasium, which was built around the same time. (FEW.)

Cars are driving along Randall Boulevard as men stand in formation on Argonne Parade Field. Soldiers utilized the parade grounds throughout the day. In the background, several of the houses on Officers' Row can be seen. On the left is the post's flagpole. (FEW.)

Pictured is Officers' Row. On the left are five duplex quarters, and then a single officer's quarters, Building No. 91. With 5,940 square feet, Quarters No. 91 was built for the field-grade officer's family and was completed May 5, 1910, for $16,181.38. The structure has 30 windows, wooden floors, and a tiled roof. Quarters Nos. 92 and 93 are in the background. (FEW.)

Officers' Row housing runs along the Argonne Parade Field. The next-to-last residence on the left is Quarters No. 92, which housed the commander, the highest ranking officer on the base, and his family. The architect who designed the Historic Governors' Mansion in Cheyenne also designed these quarters. The structure cost $26,552.05 to build on May 5, 1910, and had 5,142 square feet. (FEW.)

This is an early-1900s aerial view of the base with Cheyenne in the background. The main connecting road is Pershing Boulevard, named after Gen. John Pershing. The diamond shape in the foreground is the original parade field with Officers' Row on the left. On the right of the main road are the barracks with the stables and railroad tracks behind and Crow Creek to the right of them. (WSA.)

This residential area consisting of 325 buildings was built in 1952. There were five different designs for single-family and two different ones for duplex quarters. They all had only one story and were made from concrete blocks on concrete slabs, with shallow-gabled or flat tar-and-gravel roofs. The structures were torn down in the 1990s. (FEW.)

Four

Famous or Infamous People

Troops Assigned to the Base or People Who Lived in Housing

These unidentified members of a state flag honor guard marched in the parade on July 22, 1890, to commemorate Wyoming being admitted as the 45th state. The young ladies in this picture are in Company K; the other such unit was Company I. These women make up the first all-female guard unit in the United States. An unidentified man's image is in the upper left corner. (WSA.)

Brig. Gen. David Allen Russell, a volunteer in the 8th Infantry, fought in the Civil War. He was killed during the Third Battle of Winchester. When Russell was a captain, Gen. William Sherman, then a lieutenant, worked for him. General Sherman named the Army posts in the West and commemorated the life of General Russell by naming the new post in Dakota Territory Fort D.A. Russell. (FEW.)

Wyoming's last territorial governor and first statehood governor was Francis Emroy Warren. He then went on to become one of Wyoming's two senators, an office that he held for 37 years until his death. He was instrumental in improving the quality of life for the military, and following his death in November 1929, the post was named after him. His son-in-law was Gen. John Pershing, the only man ever named in his lifetime as General of the Armies and second only to George Washington in historical US military rank. When Captain Pershing married Miss Frances Warren, Senator Warren stated "that only a general could keep his daughter in the lifestyle she had become accustomed to," and within six months Pershing went from captain to general with Senator Warren's support. (WSA.)

Music was an important aspect of military life, providing support to marching soldiers and entertainment to the post. Shown is a nine-piece military band of unidentified soldiers from the field artillery in July 1926. (WSA.)

The unidentified bandleader is surrounded by 29 other members of an all-black band, the 9th Cavalry Band, during 1911–1912. The 9th Cavalry was an all-black unit designated in the Civil War and commonly known as a buffalo soldier unit. (WSA.)

Pvt. Chester Kasclashi, a member of Battery F in the 834th Division of the Field Artillery, is wearing a "1918" uniform, which was the style worn during World War I and commonly associated with the doughboy. Jodhpurs and a campaign hat were the identifying features of this uniform. (WSA.)

An unidentified cavalry officer is sitting at a desk with inkwells and pens placed conveniently. Electricity was installed on the post in the early 1900s, many years after being installed in Cheyenne, one of the first cities to have electric streetlights, in the 1880s. (WSA.)

Standing in front of the Headquarters Building, Building No. 210, are, from left to right, Dr. Jeserum, Lieutenant Colonel Cannon, Lt. Col. J.L. Torrey, Maj. James Harboard, Major Wheeler, and Col. Bob Caverley. These six men represent the top-ranking officers on the post during the 1890s. (WSA.)

Dewey Forgerson, wearing his protective leather apron, was the blacksmith for the 1st Infantry in 1927. The Army sent its blacksmiths to farrier training at Mounted Service School in Fort Riley, Kansas, for four months. This gentleman was the caretaker for Pole Mountain Maneuvers Camp after the last horse left the post in 1943. (FEW.)

The procurement office was named best 1962–1963 Strategic Air Command and best in the Fifteenth Air Force. From left to right are Col. E.B. Daily, 1st Lt. Gerald E. Martin, Layle B. Nelson, and Brig. Gen. William S. Rader, the 13th Strategic Missile Division commander. At the end of the rating period, the base was reassigned from the Fifteenth to the Eighth Air Force. (WSA.)

Col. Arthur Rodgers was the commander of the 90th Bomb Group during World War II in the South Pacific. The patch has skull and "cross bombs," instead of crossbones. In 1963, the 90th Missile Wing was designated after the World War II 90th Bomb Group. The four squadrons are named after the original squadrons—319th, 320th, 321st, and 400th. (FEW.)

Unidentified soldiers are recovering in the Post Hospital, Building No. 31, during the 1920s. Sparse furnishing was common for hospitals. Even so, there are several rocking chairs for patients to enjoy. The hospital was the last place where soldiers wanted to be lying in a bed all day. (WSA.)

Unidentified men, encouraged to take in fresh air daily in order to aid in their recovery, are taking it easy, recovering on the porch of the Post Hospital (Building No. 31), and enjoying coffee and bottled beer. Those who smoked took the opportunity to do so while outside. This photograph was taken between 1900 and 1920. (WSA.)

At military funerals to honor fallen comrades, the military offers a three-volley salute with M1 Garand rifles at the cemetery service. Normally, such a salute involves any number of men shooting three rounds, but at this 1944 funeral, one soldier is clearly missing from the lineup. Men competed for their spots in the honor guard and wore their dress uniforms. (FEW.)

US military funerals always have flags draped on caskets as well as three-volley salutes. Also evident in this 1935 funeral are changes in transportation. Here, members of the military are mounted on horseback, while unidentified civilians are arriving via motorized vehicles. (FEW.)

Five

Off-Duty R&R

Entertaining Life on the Plains

Here are unidentified members of Company C of the 20th Infantry enjoying a Christmas meal in 1928. Each was given menu printed in color as a remembrance of a special holiday meal. (WSA.)

A close-up of the tables shows that each man would have a program, fresh fruit, nuts, a package of Camel cigarettes, and a cigar. Each table has a bottle with dried flowers. Crepe paper was a common form of decoration at that time and was wrapped around the room's columns. (WSA.)

An artillery squad room is decorated for a festive Christmas with the unit flag on the back wall along with several wheeled cannons framing the bandstand. The room has wooden floors and pressed tin ceiling tiles, which have been painted. Normal use of the room would not have looked so festive. (WSA.)

Christmas dinner for Battery C, 4th Field Artillery, in 1910 is decorated with a foreign howitzer as a centerpiece with a display of the company trophies. Pride was taken in each of the units for any competition that might have been won and would have been displayed. Tables are set with military precision, with cups stacked six high for each table. (WSA.)

An unidentified enlisted man is standing in the decorated Thanksgiving mess hall waiting for the soldiers to enter to eat their holiday meals. On the tables are white tablecloths, pumpkin pie, gravy boats, butter, fresh fruit, and plates with sliced bread. Men would sit on either chairs or Army-designed stools, which were a common sight in the chow halls. (FEW.)

Unidentified families were encouraged to have holiday meals with soldiers. Children were especially enjoyed by all. The stools on the left were used by soldiers in the 1800s. One such stool is on exhibit at the Warren ICBM and Heritage Museum. This photograph was taken June 28, 1958. (FEW.)

Unidentified soldiers and guests are eating a Thanksgiving feast in the 1940s. Each received a printed menu listing foods served and the names of the men in the unit. This meal consisted of steamed oysters, cream of tomato soup with croutons, ham, roast turkey, chestnut dressing, buttered onions, cranberry sauce, mashed potatoes, fried celery, cold asparagus with vinaigrette sauce, fresh fruit, pumpkin pie, apple pie, nuts, milk, and coffee. (FEW.)

Occasionally, the highest-ranking person assigned to the base had a reception for members of the military to celebrate the holidays. Unidentified military officers in dress uniforms shake hands with the general assigned to the base on New Year's Eve day. The picture was taken in 1956 in the formal living room of Quarters No. 92. Area rugs have been paired with floral drapes. (FEW.)

This is the dining room of Company L, 2nd Regiment, prior to the tables being cleaned up after soldiers enjoyed Thanksgiving Day on November 20, 1941, just weeks before the December 7, 1941, the start of World War II for America. Soldiers usually sat on benches with three potbelly stoves to heat the room during the meal. (FEW.)

Pictured is the base library from the 1950s. Though there is a slight homey look with the addition of plants to the coffee tables and area rugs, the reading chairs are still lined up with military precision. Above the hot water radiator are then stylish colored curtains in a geometric print. (FEW.)

Relaxing here are two unidentified airmen reading magazines in the dayroom in the 1950s. Both are wearing green fatigue uniforms; the one on the left is a staff sergeant, and the other on the right is an airman, as he is wearing one stripe. There are linoleum floors and no rugs, as this made cleaning easier for the military. Everyone pitched in to keep buildings clean. (FEW.)

Below the new Service Club, in the basement, a poolroom was set up for men to enjoy on May 21, 1958. Chairs have been provided for those players just talking or waiting for their turns to shoot. In the background are two cigarette machines, as the military did not have any rules for smoking in buildings and even gave smoke breaks to personnel. (FEW.)

This March 21, 1958, photograph of the interior at the new Service Club shows a brick fireplace invitingly set up for people to enjoy a warm fire. Throughout the room on the tables are numerous ashtrays for smokers. It was not until the end of the 20th century that the military banned smoking in public buildings located on the base. (FEW.)

Fresh food was so scarce that everyone had gardens, including all the military companies assigned to the post. As seen in this May 1888 photograph, everyone worked the gardens, including children. Many "company" gardens were hidden from others in order to avoid stolen produce. In the background are the captains quarters at Russell, built in 1885. (WSA.)

Four unidentified soldiers are in picturesque Vedauwoo, Wyoming, just west of the post near the Pole Mountain Maneuvering range. This area is very unique and is known for the world-class "heel-and-toe" rock climbing in which no equipment is worn to aid in climbing. The name *Vedauwoo* is an Arapaho word meaning "land of the Earthborn Spirit." (FEW.)

A private was paid $19.40 a month, which he used for such expenses as haircuts, 25¢ for laundry, or a 25¢ donation to the Old Soldier's Home. Pictured during World War II are four unidentified soldiers enjoying Hamms beers purchased with part of their pay. Most men were single, as marriage was not allowed without permission from company commanders. The penalty for infraction of this rule was removal from the service. (FEW.)

Here are three unidentified cooks taking a break while drinking Schlitz and Budweiser beers during the 1940s. Drinking on the job was not allowed, but after hours, drinking in the workplace was allowed. Generally, soldiers would move to either the Noncommissioned Officer's Club or Officer's Club, depending upon their ranks. (FEW.)

During the 1920s, the post's movie theater could easily seat over 350 people in the wooden fold-down seats. The two windows on each side of the screen were not typical of most movie theaters. (WSA.)

The post's chapel is doubling as a movie theater, as evident in the back left side of the photograph. Unidentified nurses, soldiers, patients, children, and wives of soldiers are enjoying the movie while sitting on pews and benches. This photograph was taken between 1910 and 1930. (WSA.)

The unidentified 76th Field Artillery, Black Horse Battery, completes a mock charge during the rodeo at Cheyenne Frontier Days in 1915. This special elite unit allowed only black horses. In 1912, Benjamin O. Davis Sr. rode atop six racing horses "Roman" style, demonstrating his extensive riding skills to the audience of Cheyenne Frontier Days. (WSA.)

During a rodeo at Cheyenne Frontier Days, unidentified men from the 14th Cavalry on horseback and members of a military band are marching on the racetrack. The military has been a part of the event's grand entry for over 100 years, as military cannons have marked the start of each rodeo. To this day, a cannon is shot to officially start the rodeo and once again to start the wild-horse race. (WSA.)

The first Cheyenne Frontier Days was held in September 1897. The military has been a part of the celebration since that time. This was a typical sight during the rodeo as the military would demonstrate to entertain the audience in between the rodeo acts. The unidentified troops of 14th Cavalry are riding in the rodeo grounds in the 1920s. (WSA.)

Women were officially allowed to join the military in World War II. Here, bleachers have been set up for visitors to Cheyenne Frontier Days in the 1950s. In the foreground is a female military unit marching and preparing to salute the officers in the stands. (FEW.)

The 17th Infantry Band is marching in 1888 on the original diamond-shaped parade field, now named Marne Parade Field. Children from the post enjoyed following the music provided by the band. In the background are the dollhouses, which were built in 1885 and are the oldest structures still standing on the installation. (FEW.)

Members of this 30-piece band from the 9th Cavalry, along with two of its mascots, are sitting on the porch of the barracks holding their instruments. The conductor is standing to the left by the kettle drum. Clarinets, saxophones, trumpets, oboes, French horns, tubas, snare drums, and a base drum were all played by these unidentified men. (WSA.)

In 1925, the post allowed student cadets to train and exercise. Here, unidentified cadets are exercising with rifles to become comfortable with carrying and holding a weapon. This practice helps them learn to work in formation as a one-unit team. This tradition of supporting students continues on to the present day, as the headquarters for the Wyoming Wing Civil Air Patrol is located on base. (WSA.)

Nona B. Donovan, an Army nurse stationed at the post in 1920, is riding a horse for exercise. She is wearing knee-high riding boots, carrying a crop, and wearing gauntlet gloves for protection. Donovan is also wearing a hat; up until the 1960s, many women always wore a hat when they were outdoors. (WSA.)

The first female governor in the United States, Wyoming's Nellie Tayloe Ross, throws the ball for polo on Argonne Parade Field with an unidentified officer and polo players. Polo was played, indoors and outdoors, by Gen. (then captain) Billy Mitchell in 1912. General Mitchell is known as the "Father of Air Power" and the "Father of the Air Force." The last polo match played on the installation was in 1986. (WSA.)

The installation has played polo on base since the 1800s. The last game was played on Argonne Parade Field in 1986 at a match held in July during Cheyenne Frontier Days. Unidentified Cheyenne Polo Club players and an opposing team are in a battle for the polo ball in front of Officers' Row. (FEW.)

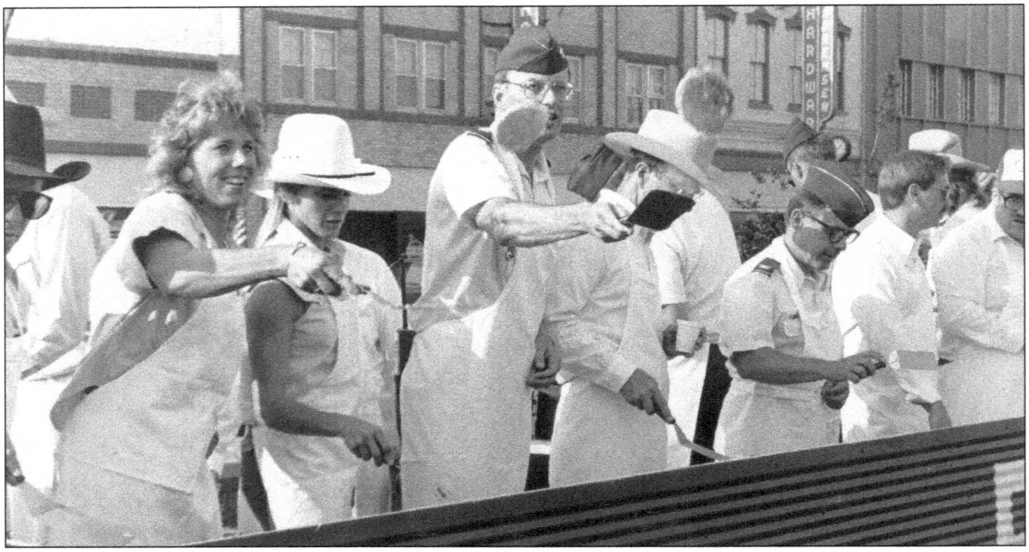

In 1988, dignitaries help cook flapjacks for a free pancake breakfast during Cheyenne Frontier Days. Unidentified people are helping Col. John Gordon, the 90th Strategic Missile Wing commander (center), and to the right Gov. Mike Sullivan, Colonel Seniawaski and Mayor Don Erickson. The tradition of being a "flapjack-flipper" has been an honor for many years. The breakfast was used for training in disaster-preparedness. During one of the three Kiwanis-sponsored breakfasts, it was not unusual to feed over 10,000 within several hours. The pancake mix was placed in new cement trucks and mixed for the meal (FEW.)

In 1910, the football championship was won by unidentified members of M Company of the US Engineers. Turtleneck sweaters along with bloused knickerbockers and striped socks are worn with high-top cleated shoes. Football was played early on by those in the military. (WSA.)

A group of unidentified men in football uniforms is posing for a picture on Argonne Parade Field with part of Officers' Row in the background. Most of the cottonwood trees are still very young in this picture. Also, the team members are wearing some padding under their colorfully striped jerseys, along with leather helmets. (WSA.)

Unidentified members of D Battalion of the 4th Field Artillery held a boxing match on October 21, 1911. Their boxing ring was a rope tied between four columns with a cloth thrown down. Boxing was a common sport in the military, and each unit took pride in its best boxer. (WSA.)

Sitting on the steps of a barracks are members of the 9th Cavalry baseball team. In 1912, they won the championship of the Fort Russell Baseball League against the 11th Infantry, 4th Artillery, Company I of the Signal Corps and the Hospital Corps. (WSA.)

In 1925, unidentified members of Battery C of Company 76th Field Artillery baseball team won the championship. Even in 1925, baseball players wore cleated lace-up shoes. The gentleman in the center of the second row proudly holds the unit guidon with its crossed cannons, which was an artillery insignia that was worn on the collars of their uniforms. (WSA.)

These are members of a cavalry baseball team on July 1, 1926. The group is still in uniform, even though the catcher is wearing baseball protective gear. Many men enjoyed the opportunity to play sports, and the military encouraged participation from the soldiers in the units. (WSA.)

In the 1940s, four unidentified men and one unidentified woman took time off to fish and caught over 40 brook trout by fly-fishing. West of the post are Granite Springs and Crystal Lake Reservoirs adjacent to Pole Mountain. (FEW.)

Not only were baseball, football, and boxing played by men at the post, but basketball was also enjoyed. Unidentified members of the 76th Field Artillery were the 1925 basketball champions. The post had several different basketball courts on which soldiers could play. (WSA.)

Chaplain James G. de la Vergne (left) and Martha Procter were a mixed doubles tennis team in 1938. Procter had been living in Hawaii, had won the women's singles, and was a member of the mixed doubles champion team in Hawaii. De la Vergne was singles champion of Fort Warren. (WSA.)

Six

No Hunting from the Barracks Windows

Military Horses, Dogs, and Other Animals on Base

Dogs have not only been mascots, but have been used by the military to detect illegal drugs, bombs, and other activities. The base has been home to the 90th Security Forces Military Working Dog section since the early 1970s. Nowadays, military dogs are deployed. Through their heroic deeds, many human lives have been saved. Pictured are an unidentified dog and man demonstrating how a dog would stop someone from fleeing. (FEW.)

This unidentified blacksmith was responsible for reviewing each mule and horse in three different ways to determine if new shoes were needed. First he checked for wear on the old shoe, second watched the horse in motion to see if movement needed improved, and last determined the shape and position of the hoofs while standing. Hundreds of mules were used on post to move supplies and pull caissons and cannons. (WSA.)

Hitched mules are pulling the machine guns of Company Q in a 1927 parade review on the original parade field. Even though mules were said to be stubborn animals, they did not need the special feed that horses required to maintain a healthy body. (WSA.)

This horse barn, built between 1904 and 1910, has carriage bumpers on the corners of the building and in the doorways, as can be seen at the bottom of each double door. They protect the buildings from wagon wheels, as the wheels would slide off of the bumpers instead of taking out part of the building. Through the doorway are safety chains connected to stop run away horses. (WSA.)

An unidentified trooper dressed in winter gear is holding a haltered horse in midwinter during the 1920s. If one looks carefully, the outline of a saddle with a breast collar is visible in the horse's hair. His ribs are showing, reflecting his hard use; consequently, this animal would probably be seen by a veterinarian and be given extra food rations to put on some weight. (WSA.)

Military men were encouraged to work on their horsemanship through competitions. Horse jumping was one such event. Here, an unidentified soldier holds a saddled horse under a wooden jump at the entrance of the indoor exercise hall, which was used to keep horses in shape year -round during the 1920s. (WSA.)

Unidentified mounted cavalrymen of Company E jump horses over a fence in formation. Gen. George B. McClellan designed these more streamlined McClellan military saddles commonly used during the late 1800s and early 1900s. The Army chose the McClellan saddle because of its cost-cutting style and serviceability. Anyone who rode on this saddle would agree that the design catered to the comfort of the horse rather than that of the trooper. (WSA.)

Pack Train No. 24 is loaded with supplies leaving Fort Russell just before it headed to Cuba during the Spanish-American War in 1898. Supplies were very important to the military way of life, and care was taken in the packing of the pack train. Careful watch was kept on the animals carrying the supplies, and replacements would trail with the group. (WSA.)

This cavalry horse in a winter coat of hair is held by an unidentified cavalryman dressed in denim fatigues. Notice the neck hair has been trimmed. All the livestock were taken care of throughout every season, with much time spent currying the animal's hair, just as much care was given to all the saddles, bridles, and other tack worn by the animals when they were working. (WSA.)

Horses were the primary mode of transportation and were allowed to graze while tied to a picket line by soldiers for safekeeping when a corral was not available to hold the animals overnight. On the left, Sibley tents, which were used by the Army, can be seen. These tents were patterned after the Native American teepee. (FEW.)

A pair of horses is hitched to an 1892 regulation US Army pattern ambulance. Stretchers are strapped on each side of the ambulance for convenience when they are needed. The wagon is equipped with two lamps for night travel, allowing the driver to better see the terrain, and in back is an attached step for ease in loading the wagon with wounded soldiers. (WSA.)

Cavalry horses are saddled with campaign gear, including sabers, rifles, and bedrolls. They have just been unloaded from the train in the background. Troopers are checking gear to make sure everything is ready to ride before mounting their horses. (WSA.)

Storage wagons have tongues attached and are waiting to be hitched to a team of horses. This was the Army's method of moving supplies throughout the West from one post to another or moving supplies needed to fight during the Indian Wars of the 1860s through the 1890s. (FEW.)

These horses have been tethered to a rope to allow them to graze while waiting to be loaded with supplies that were off-loaded from the train by the troopers. Soldiers would eventually trail the horses tied together. This was one method of moving supplies without the use of wagons. (WSA.)

SSgt. Richard DelaRosa watches his military working dog, Mack J105, run through an obstacle on the Security Police Dog Training Course, on April 20, 1981. Some dogs work for well over 10 years. All are honored by the military by allowing the dogs to be adopted, and the military retires them to good homes. The canine service is a popular career choice, and many soldier hope to one day have the opportunity to work with these animals. (FEW.)

In the first half of 20th century, the post offered weekly Sunday hunting trips for anyone interested in hunting. As can be seen here, this man was successful. In modern times, these animals are protected. (FEW.)

Wildlife has been found in abundance on base over the years. There is presently a small herd of deer located on the property. These animals are not hunted and are cared for by the National Resources, which is a section of the F.E. Warren Air Force Base Civil Engineer Squadron. (FEW.)

Units were allowed to have a mascot, which gave the soldiers the opportunity to have a four-legged friend. Shown here in December 1915 are unidentified men from companies E through H of the 12th Cavalry. Seen in the position of honor is a dog, this unit's mascot. (WSA.)

Mascots were well loved by the soldiers, and when a very special dog passed away, it was treated with dignity and buried with a headstone. These little graves are located in the rear courtyard of building No. 248. The grave on the right in the picture is marked by an engraved granite headstone: "1st Sgt. / Rags / Service Battery / Mascot / 1922–1938." (WSA.)

Through an agreement with the Wyoming Game and Fish Department, the pronghorn, which locals call an antelope, is a common sight. In the late 1980s, a rare albino pronghorn was born and lived to adulthood on base until its death when it crossed over Interstate 25 and was hit by a car. Those who remember him often question if he had albino descendants. (FEW.)

Troops stationed at Warren remember a sign posted in one of the barracks stating that there was to be "no hunting buffalo from the second floor of the barracks." No one knows when the sign was removed, but soldiers who were stationed at the base in the last 40 years still talk about it. (FEW.)